Healthy Eats
Sattvik Style

A collection of low fat, low carb, low sugar/salt vegetarian recipes Inspired by Ayurveda and Sattvik lifestyle

By

Ravi Devarakonda

Table of Contents

THIS BOOK IS DEDICATED TO MY DEAR FAMILY. THANK YOU JAYANTHI AND POOJA FOR PROOF READING AND SIDHARTH FOR BEING THERE.

Introduction

I learned it the hard way. Skinny physique doesn't always equate to a healthy body. Either through genetic inheritance or lifestyle choices, cholesterol, hypertension and diabetes could creep up on you as you enter middle age. This is called the metabolic syndrome. Cholesterol and hypertension are silent killers. Without regular health checkups and the absence of any symptoms, they are hard to detect. Diabetes is a different beast altogether. If you are prone to this disease, you can only delay it by changing your lifestyle. Unlike the other two, it is hard to miss the symptoms and more so to ignore them. These three create a deadly combination by working together. For example, elevated blood glucose levels thickens the blood and increases triglycerides, so the heart has to pump harder, thereby increasing hypertension. Increased LDL and triglycerides are also known to cause blood clots which is a major cause of a stroke. If ignored, these diseases can progressively degenerate and incapacitate your body. You have a choice between completely depending on medications or taking action early on to delay the onset of these ailments and leading a quality life.

Now for the good news: we live in a time where awareness about these ailments is prevalent and a multitude of choices and options to improve our lifestyles exists. Regular medical checkups and a routine that includes some physical activity, a healthy diet, and stress management techniques will greatly help you have a healthy and active livelihood.

Okay, so what are your options? Which path should you take? Who should you listen to? We all have these questions. There are a large number of experts who recommend and promote numerous ways to help you lead a healthy life. They are all good, meaningful recommendations that work for some and not so much for others. The hard part is picking one regimen and sticking to it till the end. I believe that *if you are kicking and forcing yourself to do a certain activity then you are destined to fail*. You should pick an activity and a lifestyle that becomes a second nature to you and you feel great following it.

After trying out different regimens and diets, they got me thinking. Why do we have this health epidemic more so in the 20th century and not so much until 100 years ago? Clearly modernization and globalization has something to do with this. The abundance of processed food combined with reduced physical activity and increased stress levels is wreaking havoc on our bodies. To find the answer to this, let us go back a few centuries and study what our ancestors were doing right. You will come across "Ayurveda", the natural way of treating ailments and "Sattvik" lifestyle as wonderful choices that have been proven to be effective over centuries. I am trying to gather and compile any useful information and techniques that I have tried for myself from this vast reservoir of knowledge and hope to pass it on to people who are interested in trying something new.

This book doesn't profess 100% Sattvik living. It is simply not feasible to follow a strict Sattvik regimen with our current lifestyles. I have merely drawn inspiration from Ayurveda/Sattvik living and combined that knowledge with my experimentation of creating new recipes using ingredients that are fresh, vegetarian, organic, raw, and unprocessed. My dishes are made of most vegetables available in North America which include a wide variety available in Asia as well. Of all the regional cuisine, my family loves Mediterranean the most. It comes close to Sattvik style, good to taste and proven to be the best diet to lower cardiovascular related diseases in medical studies. I also add a healthy dose of Latin American, Southeast Asian and of course Indian cuisine. I have spent countless hours watching cooking shows, researching on the net, exchanging ideas with likeminded friends and family; I experimented and tried out the recipes many times to improvise and master the taste. I started a page on Facebook called "Sattvik Living by Ravi Devarakonda" in 2012. The steady increase in the number of responses and page visits encouraged me to take it to this next level. Although Facebook gives me gratification and flexibility to add new recipes instantly, this book allows me to share more details on additional facts which help understand the ingredients and their power on our palate as well as our bodies.

Finally, I do not profess to be a life coach, a certified dietician or a great cook, but my intention is to share what I have discovered in the quest to fight ailments like diabetes and high blood pressure by changing my diet to lead a healthy life. I am also encouraged by the fact that healthy dieting is contagious. I have seen how it affects my friends and family and how enthusiastic they are to adopt this diet. I am hoping that you will find my book useful and if you do, please tell a friend.

How this book is put together

This book starts with a brief explanation of what "Sattvik" means. My focus is to delve into leading a healthy life through the Sattvik diet. An artist is only as good as his/her tools. Cooking is no different. The kitchen is your canvas, utensils are your brushes, and ingredients are your colors. Hence, I start with basic requirements of kitchen equipment, their maintenance, and basic cooking techniques. Most of you may be well aware of these methods, but I have to address novices as well as experts alike. Next, I group recipes into salads, soups, snacks, main courses, and desserts, followed by a list of ingredients with their nutritional values. Lastly, I have included explanations to some health terms you will come across frequently.

What is Sattvik Lifestyle?

"Sattva" is an ancient Sanskrit term that means harmony, clarity, and balance.

The three attributes (gunas) – *Sattva*, *Rajas* and *Tamas*, exist intrinsically in all of the things in nature (and in the mind). *Sattvik*, or pure, is the ideal state of mind, because a person with this quality is calm, alert, kind, and thoughtful. A person whose mind is predominantly *Rajasik* (too active/dynamic) always seeks diversions (incessant activity). The *Tamasik* mind is a dull, lethargic mind steeped in laziness and ignorance.

Eating *Sattvik* food and following a *Sattvik* lifestyle was (and still is), according to Ayurveda, a major goal in the pursuit of optimal physical and mental health. This concept of healthy eating and healthy living that existed thousands of years ago in India is remarkably relevant today!

Cooking Basics

Knives & Cutting Board:
Half the time of cooking is spent in preparing the vegetables such as rinsing, peeling, and chopping. Having the proper tools make this job easier and lot more fun.

Cutting Board
Invest in a good quality cutting board. A bamboo cutting board is ideal. It does not dull the knife's sharpness, inhibits germ growth, and lasts longer. Never put any kind of wooden boards in the dishwasher. The wet and dry cycle will warp and crack the wood. Just clean them under running water with mild soap or even simply wipe it with a wet cloth. I prefer to have a separate small board and knife just for fruits so you don't have to eat garlicky apples.

Knives
I cannot insist enough on having set of good quality knives along with a knife sharpener. It reduces your prep time. I have noticed cutting onion with a sharp knife doesn't make you cry so much. I recommend a 7" chef's knife with a smooth edge for most of the cutting, a medium serrated knife for chopping tomatoes and such, a small knife for more delicate hand held jobs such as peeling. The advantage of having a smooth edge is you can sharpen it on a regular basis and use it for a long time. Serrated knives are good for a while, but cannot be sharpened effectively later.

Cooking pasta
Dry pasta has long shelf life and makes a quick dish when you are lazy or out of ideas. Overcooked pasta is too soft and increases its glycemic index. Pasta or spaghetti should be cooked "al Dante", meaning "firm to the bite". This stage occurs when the whiteness at the center disappears. Pasta should be cooked in a large pot with a lot of water to give it room to cook properly and get rid of excess starch when drained.

Bring the water to a boil. Add a spoon of salt and add the pasta. Depending on your stove power it may take 15 to 20 minutes to cook. Keep checking by removing one pasta and cutting a piece of it. Continue until the center has no whiteness. Serve with sauce to eat it as soon as possible. If you are not ready for the next stage, wash with cold water to stop the cooking process. Alternatively, as done in restaurants, half cook your pasta, drain, and keep aside. Just before adding it to the sauce, drop it in boiling hot water for a few more minutes to complete the rest of the cooking.

Tip: Save the hot water after draining the pasta. Drop in chopped carrots, broccoli, and other vegetables until they are soft but crunchy to bite. Mix with your pasta sauce.

Cooking Bulgur/Quinoa:

Cooking bulgur or quinoa is very similar to cooking rice.

Bulgur: Bulgur comes in mainly three grades or sizes, 1 being the smallest and 3, the largest. Size 1 and 2 are used for salads and require little cooking. Add 1.5 cups of boiling water to 1 cup of bulgur and let it absorb completely.

For #3, add 1 cup of bulgur to 2 cups of water and cook in medium heat until the water is fully absorbed (about 20 minutes).

Quinoa: Toast one cup of seeds in a pan on medium heat for 5 minutes to bring out the nutty flavor. Add two cups of water or stock and cook until the water is gone. Toasting is optional.

I prefer combining half cup quinoa to 1 cup of bulgur and cook with 3 cups of water.

Cooking Steel cut Oats

Method 1: Bring 4 cups of water to a boil, add a pinch of salt, and add 1 cup of oats. Reduce heat and cook for 20 minutes, mixing occasionally to make sure it doesn't stick. Add more water if you prefer thin oatmeal.

Method 2: This is an easier way if you are going to eat the next day. Add 1 cup of oats to 4 cups of boiling water, bring to boil, reduce heat, cover and cook for 5 minutes and remove from flame. Transfer to a closed serving dish after cooling it and refrigerate. This makes 4 portions and preserves well for up to two weeks in the refrigerator.

Soups

My Signature soup with Acorn Squash

What you need:

Acorn Squash	1
Onion	1 big
Carrot	3 large
Celery	3 stalks
Fennel Bulb	1
Beans of your choice	1 can
Barley	½ cup
Tomatoes	2
Tomato paste	1 tsp
Sun dried tomatoes in Olive Oil	
Leek	1
Vegetable stock or water	6 cups
Basil leaves	2

Peel and roughly chop the veggies except tomatoes. For the fennel bulb, remove the base and the part just above the bulb, and chop. Slice the leek vertically and rinse thoroughly in a bowl of water to remove any grit, and then chop.

Heat a large pot, add two spoons of Extra Virgin Olive Oil (EVOO), add veggies, sprinkle with salt and pepper and fry for 5 minutes.

Add stock, two whole tomatoes, and a spoon of tomato paste and bring to a boil. Reduce heat to medium heat, and add barley or beans and cover.

After about 30 minutes, remove and peel the tomatoes, and then add to a blending bowl along with a piece of ginger, garlic clove, sun dried tomatoes, and some of the soup mix with veggies, basil and blend.

Add to soup, adjust seasoning, cover on simmer for 2 minutes and you're done.

Let the soup stand in the pot for another 10 minutes before serving.

TIPS AND TRICKS:

THERE IS NO ONE WAY TO MAKE A PERFECT SOUP. THERE ARE SO MANY VEGETABLES YOU CAN ADD TO A SOUP BUT TRY TO KEEP IT TO A MINIMUM. ONION, CARROT, AND CELERY FORMS THE BASE FOR THESE KIND OF SOUPS SO REMEMBER THE ITALIAN (OR INDIAN) FLAG COLORS.

YOU CAN ADD A SPOON OF ALL-PURPOSE FLOUR WHEN FRYING THE VEGETABLES WHICH GIVES A NICE TEXTURE TO THE LIQUID.

DO NOT FRY LONG ENOUGH TO CHAR THE VEGGIES, LEST IT CHANGES THE SOUP'S COLOR AND TASTE.

SAVE THE SQUASH SEEDS, ADD A SPOON OF EVOO, PINCH OF SALT AND TOAST UNTIL LIGHT GOLDEN BROWN. GARNISH THE SOUP WITH THESE SEEDS AND LEAVES FROM FENNEL BULB (SIMILAR TO DILL) AS SHOWN IN THE ABOVE PICTURE.
ADD ANY FRESH HERBS **AFTER** YOU TURN OFF THE HEAT. COOKING AFTER ADDING ANY FRESH HERBS IS A BIG NO-NO.

DON'T MIX MORE THAN TWO FRESH HERBS. YOUR PALATE WILL BE LEFT CONFUSED.

POTATOES AND CARROTS ARE A GREAT SOURCE OF POTASSIUM. IF YOU PEEL THEM, YOU LOSE MOST OF IT. I SCRUB THEM WITH MILD SOAP.

ADD PASTA 10 MINUTES BEFORE TURNING OFF THE HEAT. SHELLS, ROTINI, ELBOWS OR TUBES WILL WORK BETTER.

COMPLIMENT THEM WITH A THICK LOAF OF ROSEMARY BREAD AVAILABLE IN MOST GOURMET MARKETS AND YOU GOT YOURSELF A COMPLETE MEAL. TOAST THE BREAD WITH A LITTLE EVOO FOR BEST RESULTS.

CONSIDER THE FOLLOWING VEGETABLES AS ALTERNATIVES:
POTATOES
FRESH GREEN BEANS
YELLOW SQUASH
ZUCCHINI
CHAYOTE
ANY OTHER SQUASH (UNRIPE)

Butternut Squash Soup

I love soups made out of squashes in the fall and winter. They make a perfect, hearty soup to lift your spirits on a cold, dark day. They are available in all grocery stores and lasts for weeks in your pantry. Pick a small to medium size squash with no cuts and bruises. For acorn squash, pick the greenest for less sweetness, which can ruin the soup.

What you need:

Butternut squash	1
Onion	1 small
Carrots	2
Celery	2 stalks
Ginger	½ tsp
Thyme	1 spoon

Cut the squash in the middle horizontally, remove seeds, and place the cut side down. Using a sharp knife, remove the skin and cut into cubes. If this proves to be too much for you, you can cut it lengthwise, remove seeds, sprinkle with salt and olive oil, roast in the oven at 375 degrees Fahrenheit for 30 minutes or more until it becomes fork tender. Then you can scoop the insides. Heat a spoon of olive oil on a stock pot, add diced carrots, celery, onion, and squash. Sprinkle some salt and pepper, cook for two minutes and then add 6 cups of water or low sodium vegetable stock. Bring to a boil and simmer with the cover on for 30 minutes. Add ginger and fresh thyme, and then blend using an immersion blender or a normal blender in small batches. I sometimes add fresh garlic at this stage. Adjust seasoning and serve hot.

As shown, I have served with a spoon of salsa. Also can be served with some cream and garnished with cilantro or parsley. Rinse the seeds, add a spoon of olive oil and a pinch of salt, cover in a silver foil, and toast for 10 minutes. They are great to eat directly or better yet, sprinkle on your soup or salad.

Green Lentil Soup

What you need:

Green lentils	1 cup (rinsed).
Carrots	2 big
Celery	3 stalks
Onion	1 big
Bay leaf	1
Coriander and cumin powder	1 spoon each

Add two spoons of olive oil to a hot pan, along with chopped carrots, celery, onion, bay leaf. Fry for couple of minutes. Add salt, pepper, coriander powder, cumin powder, and then add 5 cups of water or vegetable stock. Add lentils, bring to a boil, and simmer with the lid on for 30 to 40 minutes until the lentils are soft. You can add green herbs of your choice. You can puree with a hand held blender to desired consistency but I choose to just eat without that step. You can also add tomatoes in the initial stages to add color and taste.

Salads

Dressings

A good salad dressing turns chopped vegetables into a great salad. Store bought salads are packed with salt, sugar and 20 other chemicals that you may have never heard of. I want to show you a few recipes that are easy to make and taste wonderful.

Two of the primary ingredients in a dressing are oil and acid. Whisked together, the acidity breaks up the oil in a process called emulsification. I always go with extra virgin olive oil with lemon juice or vinegar for acidity. Vinegar comes in plain, balsamic, red wine, and white wine flavors.

Basic dressing

Take a round-bottomed bowl and add juice from one lemon, a pinch of salt, and pepper. Using a fork, keep whisking while slowly pouring in ½ cup of olive oil. If vinegar is used in place of lemon juice, the dressing is called vinaigrette.

Fancy balsamic vinaigrette

Mix ½ spoon of yellow or Dijon mustard, 2 minced garlic cloves, ½ spoon salt, ½ spoon honey or sugar, ½ spoon freshly ground pepper, and 3 spoons of good balsamic vinegar in a bowl. Whisk in ½ cup of olive oil and adjust the seasonings.

Fattoush salad dressing

Mix 3 cloves of minced garlic, ½ spoon salt, ½ spoon pepper, ½ spoon pomegranate concentrate (optional), 1 spoon of tahini, 2 spoons of vinegar, 2 spoons lemon juice, 1 spoon of sumac in a large bowl. Whisk 1 cup of olive oil slowly.

Carrot-Ginger dressing

Boil one medium-sized carrot. Blend it with 1 spoon of ginger, 1 spoon of brown sugar, two spoons of lite soy sauce, ½ spoon of salt, and 2 spoons of sesame oil. Add more water for the right consistency.

Arugula salad with Tahini dressing

What you need:

Tahini paste	1/3 cup
Garlic	1 clove minced
Soy sauce	4 tsp
Sugar	½ tsp
Ginger	½ tsp minced
Vinegar	2 tsp
Lemon juice	1 tsp
EVOO	1/3 cup
Pita bread	1
Arugula	3 cups packed
Sweet onion	1 medium sliced
Cucumber	1 small, sliced

Mix all of the ingredients except olive oil in a bowl. Add two spoons of water if necessary to make it smooth. Whisk extra virgin olive oil into it and adjust seasoning. Brush a pita bread with oil and toast until it's crispy. Crumble it and mix with your Arugula, tomatoes (sliced cherry would be nice), cucumber, onion, and prepared dressing. You can garnish with little crumbled feta cheese.

Arugula has a hint of bitterness and probably tastes better with a simple balsamic wine vinaigrette. For tahini dressing, romaine lettuce and baby spinach would be an excellent choice.

TIPS AND TRICKS:

YOU CAN MAKE THIS DRESSING AHEAD OF TIME AND TOSS WITH SALAD JUST BEFORE SERVING.

IF MIXED TOO SOON, THE ACIDITY WILL MAKE THE GREENS SOGGY.

LEFTOVER DRESSING CAN BE STORED IN THE REFRIGERATOR UP TO A WEEK.

TAHINI CAN BE REPLACED WITH ALMOND PASTE.

SOY SAUCE CONTAINS LOTS OF SALT, SO REDUCE THE AMOUNT OF ADDITIONAL SALT YOU MAY WANT TO ADD.

IF SWEET VIDALIA ONION IS NOT AVAILABLE, YOU CAN USE ANY OTHER ONION. IF THEY ARE TOO STRONG, SOAK THE ONION SLICES IN COLD WATER WITH ICE CUBES, ADD A SPOON OF VINEGAR AND THEN DRAIN AFTER 30 MINUTES.

Avocado Salad/Guacamole

This is a regular dish in our kitchen and kids really love it. It is super easy to make too. The key is to use the avocado at the correct ripeness. They can be hard when bought but become soft within a couple of days.

Run a knife lengthwise all around the fruit making sure the knife touches the pit inside. Using both hands, twist the two halves in opposite direction to separate. Gently tap the bottom edge of the knife on pit and twist to remove the pit. Using a spoon, scoop the insides. I sometime run the knife in crisscross lines before scooping so I don't have to cut after scooping. Sprinkle with lemon juice, salt, pepper, and extra virgin olive oil and serve immediately.

Variations:

*Add chopped onions and cilantro, and then garnish with paprika. If the fruit is too soft then mash with a fork and you've got yourself some yummy **guacamole**.*

Bean Salad

What you need:

Kidney beans	1 can
Black beans	1 can
Garbanzo or chick peas	1 can
Cilantro or parsley	½ cup
Red onion	1
Green onions	2
Red and green bell pepper	1 each

Dressing: In a bowl combine salt, fresh ground pepper, lemon juice, a pinch of sugar, lemon zest, and grated ginger. Continuously whisk while slowly pouring in ½ cup of extra virgin olive oil.

Assemble:
Finely chop onion, herbs, and bell pepper. Mix veggies and beans with the dressing, adjust seasoning, and garnish with paprika. It can be refrigerated overnight and served cold.

Variations:

I have added few mozzarella cheese cubes but they can be substituted with paneer (Indian cheese) cubes. You can go crazy with different combinations of beans, roasted or steamed vegetables, greens, nuts, and ever certain fruits. You can add cooked quinoa or bulgur to make a full meal.

Lentil Salad

What you need:

Lentils with skin	1 cup
Onion	1 medium sweet
Black beans	1 can rinsed
Flat-leaf parsley	cup
Extra virgin olive oil	¼ cup
Salt, pepper, and lemon juice to taste	

Rinse the lentils. Add enough water and bring it to a boil with a pinch of salt. Cook until it's done, making sure it's not too soft and skin is separating. Drain, rinse again with cold water and keep aside. Thinly chop the onion, add black beans, chopped parsley, salt, fresh ground pepper and the juice of one big lemon. Drizzle liberally with extra virgin olive oil and adjust the seasoning to taste. Some modifications you can make - parsley can be replaced with cilantro with hint of basil or mint leaves. Finely chopped jalapeno will add a nice kick, chopped celery will give a nice crunch. Add a mix of beans for color and texture. 1/4 spoon of grated ginger can be your secret ingredient for some extra zing.

Farro Salad

See Lentil Salad. Replace lentils with cooked Farro.

Raw Papaya Salad and Curry

Salad:

Julienned papaya	2 cups
Tomatoes	2 (cut in half, deseed, slice thinly)
Garlic	1 clove (thinly chopped)
Carrot	1 (skinned, thinly sliced)
Grated ginger	¼ spoon
Jalapeno	1 thinly sliced

Mint leaves, pinch of sugar, salt, pepper, lemon juice

Mix garlic, ginger, lemon juice, sugar, salt, pepper in bowl and add tomatoes and press gently with a flat bottomed tumbler or vessel. . Add julienned vegetables to the mix and toss to finish the salad. I substituted sugar with agave nectar due to its low glycemic index. Jalapeno can be replaced with crushed red pepper. Thai salad style uses tamarind paste instead of lemon juice. Mint gives the summer freshness to salads. You can use fresh basil, or cilantro instead.

Curry:

Raw Papaya	3 cups (cubed)
Coconut	fresh/dry/frozen or can of coconut milk
Onion	small
Garlic	2 cloves
Ginger	1/2 spoon chopped
Green chilies	4 sliced
Mustard and cumin seeds	1 spoon each

Heat a couple of spoons of oil in a wok and add green chilies. After a minute add papaya cubes, 1 cup of water, ½ spoon turmeric powder, some chopped ginger, pinch of salt and let cook covered on medium heat for 10 minutes. Meanwhile, in a mixer/grinder add coconut, mustard seeds, garlic, onion and some water and blend into a fine paste. I added some extra mustard for that "clear your sinuses" effect. Add this paste to papaya, add some more water if needed and let it cook without boiling till the onions are cooked and lose the raw smell. . Mix occasionally and adjust seasonings. After it is cooked, top it with some tempering using curry leaves, mustard seeds (again), cumin seeds and hing/asafetida (optional)

Warm Greens Salad

This is one of the best ways to eat leafy vegetables such as mustard greens, spinach, kale, Swiss chard, and collard greens. I have used chard in this picture.

What you need:

Leafy greens	1 bunch
Onion	1
Garlic	3 cloves
Crushed chili pepper	½ spoon
Olive oil	2 spoons
Lemon	1
Salt, pepper	¼ spoon each

Thoroughly rinse the leaves and chop them. Veins of chard are edible. But if you use Kale and other leafy greens which are thick, the veins need to be removed. . Heat oil in a wok add chopped garlic on low heat and fry till golden. Add chili flakes and chopped greens. Add salt, mix and cover with a lid. Cook on medium heat for about 10 minutes mixing once. The idea is not to overcook and lose all the nutrients. Sprinkle with pepper, extra virgin oil and lemon juice and serve hot or cold.

Jicama Salad

What you need:

Jicama	1 medium
Carrots	2
Radishes	4

Salt, pepper, extra virgin olive oil, lemon juice, and mint

Preparation:

Trim the top and bottom of the jicama root so you can keep it stable on the cutting board. Using a sharp knife, cut along the sides to remove a thick layer of skin. Using a peeler is not recommended because we want to remove more than top thin layer. Cut into thin strips using just the knife or a mandolin. Do the same with carrots and radishes. Mix them all in a bowl with salt, pepper, extra virgin olive oil, chopped mint, lemon juice. Sprinkle with Zaatar (see ingredients section) or sumac before serving.

Snacks/Side Dishes

Oatmeal

What you need (4 servings):

Steel cut oats	1 cup
Water	3 cups
Salt	1 pinch

Bring water to a boil and add oats. Add a pinch of salt, cook on medium heat for about 20 minutes, stirring occasionally.. You can prepare more and store in refrigerator for few days. To reheat, just add some water or milk and microwave.

Plain oatmeal is chewy and bland. You can try a myriad of combinations for toppings to make it interesting. Toasted walnuts, raisins, almonds, fresh grapes, berries, chopped apple, banana, brown sugar, honey and maple syrup just to name few. As shown in the picture, I have added peanut butter, agave nectar (natural sweetener with low glycemic value), banana, and chopped prunes (high fiber). If you love peanut butter like I do, make sure to buy the natural peanut butter, the one which contains no other ingredients but peanuts. Most brands will have hydrogenated palm oil to maintain the creamy consistency at room temperature. Natural peanut butter will have peanut oil floating on the top. To keep the oil from separating, empty the peanut butter into a bowl, mix thoroughly, put back in the bottle and refrigerate.. Note for dry fruit consumers: These tend to contain a good amount of sugars so watch out if you are diabetic.

Salsa / Pico de Gallo

What you need:

Roma Tomatoes	3
Sweet onion	1
Cilantro	1 cup
Black beans	1 can drained
Extra virgin olive oil	¼ cup
Salt, pepper, ginger, lemon juice	to taste
Chipotle peppers	1

Soak a small piece of chipotle pepper in hot water for 15 minutes. Alternately you can use chipotle pepper in adobo sauce available in cans. Drain canned beans and wash to remove extra salt and preservatives. Finely chop and mix all other ingredients except ginger. Blend softened Chipotle pepper along with the water it is soaking in with ginger. Add to the mixture and let sit for some time before serving. You can mix mango or avocado to the salad as well. This salsa can be used with chips, in sandwiches or as a garnish to soups.

Another method: Roast 1 quartered onion, 1 jalapeno pepper, 3 halved tomatoes sprinkled with salt and olive oil under broiler for 30 minutes. Coarsely blend them with a bunch of cilantro and add lemon juice.

Zucchini, yellow Squash pancakes

What you need:

Zucchini	1 medium
Yellow Squash	1 medium
Carrots	2 medium
Green onion	2 stalks, chopped
Panko bread crumbs	1 cup
Cilantro	1 cup chopped
Ginger	½ spoon minced
Salt and pepper	1 spoon each
Jalapeno pepper	1 finely chopped
Corn starch	2 spoons
Parmesan or pecorino Romano cheese	¼ cup

Using a mandolin, grate zucchini, squash, and carrots into thin slices. Mix with a spoon of salt and set it aside for 30 minutes. Take small amounts into both hands and squeeze hard to remove as much water as possible. Place it in a separate bowl and mix with rest of the ingredients. Adjust salt at this stage. Heat a pan with little oil, make small balls and press on to the pan flat. Fry till golden brown both sides (about 2 min each side). Instead of starch, you can mix 1 boiled potato to the mixture to act as a binding agent.

Roasted Potato Skins

Potatoes are a good source of complex carbs, potassium, vitamins C, and fiber. It is introduced to India in the 17th century and hence never made it to the Sattvik food list. Contrary to popular belief, potato is a healthy option for people watching their diet, provided they cook it right. Much of the fiber and antioxidants lies in and under the skin which we generally discard. You can select certain types of potatoes such as Yukon gold or red which contain thin skins that are easy to clean and consume. Potato skins are a very popular game/bar snack that are deep fried and loaded with unhealthy ingredients. I have made a healthier version here.

Preparation:

Thoroughly scrub and wash potatoes and cut into halves. Take enough water to submerge potatoes in a deep pan and bring it to a boil. Add a pinch of salt and add potatoes. Cook for about five to seven minutes, drain the water and rinse immediately with cold water to stop the cooking process. Overcooking the potato will make it fall apart and not retain the firmness. Using a melon scoop or a small spoon, remove enough of flesh to make it into a boat shape but thick enough to stand on its own. Brush all over with olive oil, sprinkle with salt, pepper, and paprika. You can add favorite seasonings such as garlic powder, Italian seasonings, cumin powder, chili powder etc., Roast them in an oven for 20 minutes. As shown in picture, I added cheese, salsa, and avocado salad.

Hummus with Roasted Red Pepper

What you need:

Red peppers	1
Chick peas (Garbanzo beans)	1 can
Tahini sauce	¼ cup (sesame paste available in stores)
Garlic	2 cloves
Extra virgin olive oil	½ cup
Lemon juice	¼ cup
Salt, pepper, paprika	

Roast red pepper on an open flame (you can also buy them in a jar) until the skin is darkened all around place it in a small container and cover tightly for 10 minutes. This allows us to peel the skin off with ease. Chop finely and set aside. You can completely skip pepper part to make traditional plain hummus but who wants plain vanilla, right? I prefer a food processor to blend the ingredients as it allows me to see the consistency and add other ingredients while it is running. So, start with garlic, tahini sauce, lemon juice and a pinch of salt and pepper, blend for two minutes until it is creamy. Now add the washed and drained chick peas (garbanzo beans) to the mix, blend for two more minutes while adding a little of olive oil and a spoon of water if necessary to make into a fine paste. Next add red pepper after saving some for garnishing. Adjust seasonings and blend for one minute. Scoop into a wide and shallow bowl, sprinkle with some paprika, drizzle a little olive oil and garnish with saved red pepper. I have also sprinkled some "Zaatar", a store bought Mediterranean spice powder mix that has dried thyme, sumac, sesame seeds, and other spices.

Hummus stores well for couple of weeks when refrigerated in a tight container. Use it as a spread on sandwiches in place of mayo, or just dip you favorite carrot sticks, broccoli, zucchini, snap peas, etc.,

To make it a bit spicy, char one jalapeno pepper over flame, remove skin and seeds and blend with the mixture.

For smoother consistency, you can rub the peas in water and remove the thin outer layer. Remember that you will be discarding some good fiber with this process.

Baba Ganoush

Fallow the above hummus recipe except replace red pepper and chick peas with *fire roasted eggplant.*

Tips:

Eggplant should be fresh so that it contains less seeds. Roast it directly over an open flame turning gentry to avoid puncturing it. After evenly charring the skin, place it in a dish and cover with silver foil for 10 minutes. This helps in peeling the skin easily and also releases some liquid which can be used while blending the mix.

Roasted Chick Peas (GARBANZO BEANS)

<u>One cup of Chickpeas</u> (chana) also known as garbanzo beans, has <u>12 grams of dietary fiber and 15 grams of protein</u> and high iron content. That is half of the daily recommended fiber which is essential in lowering cholesterol. If you are a purist and have time on your hands, soak the dry peas overnight and cook in pressure cooker or boil them until they are tender. Thankfully, they are readily available in cans and after draining and rinsing with plenty of water you can remove most of the added salt and preservatives. They also perfectly complement soups and salads.

Preparation:

Put the peas in a bowl and sprinkle with salt, pepper, two spoons olive oil, and half spoon paprika. Toss to coat evenly and spread on a baking sheet, roast under broiler for 20 minutes at 375 F. Occasionally mix the peas to spread the heat evenly. We are trying to remove the excess moisture and get nice golden brown color. In a separate bowl add finely chopped onion, green onions/scallions, half spoon chili powder (optional), lemon juice, chopped cilantro, salt, pepper, and two spoons of extra virgin olive oil. Mix the ingredients and toss with roasted peas. Serve with lemon wedges.

Variations:
You can chop and roast one jalapeno along with peas. You can also simply fry the peas instead of roasting.

Ragi (millet) Crepes

What you need:

Ragi flour	2 cups
Onion	finely chopped (1)
Green chilies	finely chopped (3)
Carrots	finely chopped (1)
Cilantro	finely chopped (1/2 cup)
Yogurt	1 spoon (Greek would be nice)
Warm water	1 cup
Salt, Fresh ground pepper	to taste

Finely chop onion, chilies, carrots and cilantro, mix with salt and pepper. Add yogurt and flour to this mix, slowly add water and knead to a dough consistency. Oil your hands and make small rounds of dough and flatten them on an oiled flat surface with your fingers. . Since it is gluten free, the dough breaks easily so don't flatten them too much. Fry on a heated pan with little oil both sides. Serve with dal or chutney. With the right spice mix, you can just eat the roti without any sides.

Variations:
You can try combinations of cumin seeds, sesame seeds, grated ginger, steamed and mashed cauliflower, chopped cabbage, grated radish, just to name a few.
You can make pancakes by adding more water and make the dough into a batter.
As shown in the picture: I have served with Greek yogurt, fresh onion and green chilies.

Oatmeal and Ripe Banana Squares

Overripe bananas, those with big black spots outside, mushy and not so sweet are begging to be thrown away, and most of us do. Not anymore. Here is a recipe using those extra ripe bananas that is fat free, low in glycemic index, high in fiber, and tasty. Peel, cut the bananas and freeze them if you want to save the bananas for future use.

What you need:

Extra ripe bananas	2
Rolled oats	1 cup
Honey or agave nectar	2 spoons
Chopped walnut	½ cup
Chopped dates	½ cup
Vanilla extract	few drops (optional)
Cinnamon powder	¼ spoon (optional)

If using frozen banana, thaw and mash them in bowl. Add rest of the ingredients and mix well. Adjust proportions to your liking if using more bananas than the recipe calls for or want to make it more sweeter/crunchier. A small pinch of salt will enhance the flavors. Spread the mix on a non-stick silver foil to about ¼ inch thickness. Bake for 25 minutes at 375 F.

You can add natural crunchy peanut butter, chia seeds, and/or amaranth seeds for extra fiber/protein and crunch.

Main Course

Stir Fry with Eggplant and Thai Basil

You can find Thai basil in most Asian stores during summer. It's inexpensive, cooks well at high temperatures compared to sweet basil.

What you need:

Thai basil	2 cups chopped
Chinese eggplant	2
Green beans	10
Carrots	2
Yellow squash	1
Zucchini	1
Onion	1
Bell pepper	1
Green onions	2

Wash the basil leaves, remove excess water, and blend in a food processor with couple of green chilies, pinch of salt and enough water to make into a thin paste. You can bottle it and store in refrigerator for a few days. For vegetables, chop these into 1 inch cubes: carrots, green beans, and eggplant, yellow squash, zucchini, onion, bell peppers, and green onions (scallions). Heat a large wok, add two spoons of lite olive oil, add veggies in the order I listed. Basic rule of thumb: harder veggies go first, greens go last. Give two minute intervals in between. Keep tossing them so as not to char them. Sprinkle with salt and pepper. I will throw in half spoon of crushed red pepper. We don't want to make them mushy; they should still have a bite to them. Add two to three big spoons of basil paste, mix well. For that authentic Thai taste, you can add a spoon of Thai chili paste and half a can of coconut milk. Bring to a boil and turn it off. Enjoy on top of noodles, rice, bulgur, or quinoa. You can be creative with vegetable selection.

Bulgur Pulihora
Recipe courtesy: Madhavi Damaraju

This is a traditional south Indian dish made with rice, tamarind extract and spices. To make it healthy, we replaced rice with bulgur, which is cracked parboiled wheat.

What you need:

Tamarind Puree	½ cup
Turmeric	2 Teaspoons
Chana dal	5-6 Teaspoons
Curry Leaves	¼ cup
Slit Green Chilies	15
Peanuts	6 tablespoons
Red Chilies whole	6-8
Mustard seeds	4 table spoons
Oil	¼ cup
Bulgur wheat or Cracked wheat	2 cups (cooked)

Pulihora Paste – Take a large pan, add oil and mustard seeds -2tbsp (keep the remaining mustard seeds aside). When mustard starts spluttering add red chilies, peanuts, chana dal, fry them until slightly golden in color. Add slit green chilies, curry leaves. Once tempering is done by above process mix concentrated tamarind puree with water and add to the pan. When this mixture is boiling add a pinch of turmeric, salt to taste then let this mixture cook until you see oil floating. Ensure to keep the flame low while cooking and mix the every couple of minutes. Adjust salt and sourness as needed.

Cook bulgur as explained in the earlier section and keep it aside.

Take the remaining mustard seeds grind for 1 min into fine powder. Don't add water or oil.

Take a large bowl add boiled cracked wheat, mustard powder and 3-4 spoons of pulihora paste. Adjust salt and sourness. Make the tempering with remaining oil, chana dal, curry leaves, and mustard seeds and add to the cracked wheat and let it rest for half an hour. This dish is best served after resting for a few hours.

Stuffed Bitter Gourd (KARELA)
Recipe inspired by: Prathima Devulapalli

A bane for children, a boon for most adults, bitter gourd has chemicals that act as antiviral, antimalarial, anticancer and helps in weight loss. But the biggest benefactor is the presence of a lectin that acts as insulin and lowers blood glucose levels. For best health benefits, these vegetable should not be overcooked. Steamed or boiled are better than frying. But today I am going to talk about a recipe that involves shallow-frying. I promise I will try steamed in the future and write about it.

Picking the right karela: Look for dark shiny green skin. It should not be too thick and not hard when you press.

What you need:

Salt	1 tsp
Turmeric	½ tsp
Peanuts	1 cup
Cumin	2 tsp
Dry red chilies	4
Yogurt	½ cup
Oil for frying	

Give a quick wash, pat dry and trim edges. For simplest curry, chop into small pieces, fry with a spoon of oil and some water cover until tender, add salt, chili powder and fry some more until done. For stuffing, make a slit lengthwise and shallow fry few minutes, add a cup of water, two spoons of yogurt, one spoon of turmeric, half a spoon salt, mix, cover until they are cooked all the way. Set them aside to cool. In a separate pan, dry roast peanuts, cumin, red chilies separately and let them cool down.

Grind dry roasted items with a spoon of salt. My trick here is if you grind when peanuts are still warm (not too warm), the blended mix will be a little sticky and stuffing won't fall off while cooking. Also I like peanuts coarsely ground for that texture.

Stuff karela with this mix and shallow fry again, carefully turning all sides to brown. You can garnish with chopped onions, cilantro. In the picture, on the side I have some bulgur and onion, radish salad with lemon juice, salt, pepper, paprika, and extra virgin olive oil.

Ingredients

Balsamic Vinegar
Made from reduction of cooked white Trebbiano grape juice. Aged balsamic vinegar is expensive but worth it. Commercial inexpensive version is widely available in stores which is made from white wine vinegar with added caramel color and other artificial flavors.

Barley
Barley is one of the earliest grains cultivated by humans. It has 8 essential amino acids and whole grain barley effectively regulates blood sugar levels for up to 10 hours after consumption due to their high levels of fiber and protein. Grains have essentially three layers not counting the top inedible husk. They are bran, germ, and endosperm. Husk is always removed before consumption. Hulled barley is just the grain with husk removed and hence a whole grain. "Pearled" barley is hull removed so it looks whiter and cooks faster. All-purpose flour is wheat with hull and germ both removed. Removing outer layers increases the glycemic index and not good for insulin tolerance.

Brussel Sprouts
This leafy vegetable from cabbage family originated from Brussels, Belgium. They are high in cancer fighting chemicals and vitamin K.

Bulgur
Durum wheat is parboiled/steamed, cooled/sundried, top inedible layer removed and then crushed into different sizes. This whole grain contains large amounts of fiber, protein and potassium. It has low glycemic index and recommended for diabetic prone people. This can be used as rice substitute.

Carom Seeds (ajwain/omam/vamu)
This is a well know herb used extensively in Ayurveda medicines and Indian dishes. It is known to reduce indigestion, flatulence, cough, and often cure asthma.

Chard and Kale
Popular leafy green vegetables containing high amounts of vitamins A, K, and C.

Chia seeds

This is a species of flowering plant from mint family cultivated mainly in South American countries. Similar to flax seed, they contain high percentage of omega-3 fatty acids and other important nutrients. They can be consumes raw sprinkled on salads, smoothies, and cereal.

Chickpeas

One cup of Chickpeas (chana) also known as garbanzo beans, has 12 grams of dietary fiber and 15 grams of protein besides high iron content. That is half of the daily recommended fiber which is essential in lowering cholesterol and keeping you full.

Chipotle peppers

Smoke-dried jalapeno peppers. Dry peppers need to be soaked in warm water with a pinch of salt for 20 minutes to reconstitute them before using. They are also available with adobo sauce in bottles/cans which are ready to be used.

Extra Virgin Olive Oil

Oil extracted from olives using cold mechanical press without using any chemical process. This is considered the highest quality of oil. After this extraction, typically the leftover paste is treated with hot water and other methods to extract remaining oil. This type is called regular or lite olive oil. Extra virgin oil is best consumed without cooking as in salads dressings. It contains large amount of monounsaturated fatty acids which is good for heart.

Green Lentils

1 cup of cooked lentils has 62% fiber and only 12% of calories your body needs in a day. It's high on both soluble and insoluble fiber content.

Oats

Oats contains more soluble fiber than any other grain and also high in protein and potassium. It is perfect food for lowering cholesterol, lose weight, and reduce blood glucose spikes. Be sure to consume steel cut oats which are unprocessed and cut with steel blade. You can also buy them as rolled oats which are steamed and rolled into flat flakes for easy cooking. This type contains less fiber than steel cut oats. Steel cut oats are available in most major grocery stores and gourmet food chain stores. Stay away from flavored instant oats.

Paprika

Paprika is the powder form of red capsicum which are either air dried or smoked.

Potato

Potatoes are a good source of complex carbs, potassium, vitamins C, and fiber. It is introduced to India in the 17th century and hence never made it to the Sattvik food list. Contrary to popular belief, potato is a healthy option for people watching their diet, provide they cook it right. Much of the fiber and antioxidants lies in the skin which we generally discard. You can select certain types of potatoes such as Yukon gold or red which contain thin skins that are easy to clean and consume.

Quinoa

Pronounced as "Qin-wah", this is a seed originally from Peru, considered as "mother of all grains" by the Incas. It's gluten-free, has high levels of protein, soluble fiber, phosphorus, magnesium, and iron.

Ragi (finger millet)

These seeds are gluten free and contain high amounts of minerals. It is widely consumed as cereals and porridge in semi-arid regions of the world.

Sumac

Sumac is powdered form of small fruits of a certain small plants grown in Mediterranean regions. It has a lemony tartness to it and widely used in salads and to garnish other dishes.

Tahini

Tahini sauce is a paste made from roasted sesame seeds and widely used in Mediterranean dishes. Store bought product is pretty decent and stores well in refrigerator.

Yam/Sweet Potato

These are starchy root vegetables with extra sweetness. Sweet potatoes have high quantities of Vitamin A and beta-carotene whereas Yams are high in Vitamin K and potassium.

Za'atar

A blend of dried spice powders from Mediterranean region. Spices include thyme, toasted sesame seeds, sumac, oregano, and other spices.

Terminology

Dietary Fiber

Also known as roughage is the indigestible portion of food derived from plants. They fall in to two categories:

> **Soluble**: dissolves in water and tend to slow the movement of food through the system. Examples – Legumes, oats, barley, root vegetables

> **Insoluble**: does not dissolve in water and tend to accelerate the movement of food through the system. Examples – Potato skins, bran, green beans, avocado

A good balance of both these fibers will keep you full for longer, controls blood glucose levels, and keeps you regular.

Protein

Protein is a nutrient needed by the human body for growth and maintenance. Vegetarian sources of proteins include legumes, nuts, seeds and fruits. Legumes, some of which are called pulses in certain parts of the world, have higher concentrations of amino acids and are more complete sources of protein than whole grains and cereals. Examples of vegetarian foods with protein concentrations greater than 7 percent include soybeans, lentils, kidney beans, white beans, mung beans, chickpeas, cowpeas, lima beans, pigeon peas, lupines, wing beans, almonds, Brazil nuts, cashews, pecans, walnuts, cotton seeds, pumpkin seeds, sesame seeds, and sunflower seeds

Carbohydrates

Carbohydrates provide your body with glucose which is converted to energy for your body to function. It is present in a wide variety of foods both healthy and non-healthy. There are three types of carbs. Starch (complex), sugar (simple), and fiber. All processed foods such as bread, ice cream, cakes, cookies, has excess amounts of simple carbs that increases your blood glucose levels. It is recommended to consume more of whole grains, nuts, beans, legumes, and fresh fruits and vegetables to get complex carbs and fiber.

Glycemic Index (GI)

This is a measure of how quickly blood glucose levels increase when a particular type of food is consumed. Glucose is given a GI of 100 and used as basis of comparison with other foods during test. Some notable examples are plain white bread (73), wheat tortilla (30), cornflakes (93), white rice (89), bulgur (48), and peanuts (7). For a list of 100 notable foods, visit the following link.

http://www.health.harvard.edu/newsweek/Glycemic_index_and_glycemic_loa d_for_100_foods.htm

Fat

Saturated:

The majority of saturated fat comes from animal products such as beef, lamb, pork poultry with skin, butter, cream, cheese and other dairy products made from whole or 2 percent milk,. All of these foods also contain dietary cholesterol. Foods from plants that contain saturated fat include coconut, coconut oil, palm oil and palm kernel oil (often called tropical oils) and cocoa butter. For people who need to lower their cholesterol, the American Heart Association recommends reducing saturated fat to no more than 5 to 6 percent of total daily calories

Unsaturated:

Polyunsaturated and monounsaturated fats are the two unsaturated fats. They're mainly found in fish such as salmon, trout and herring, avocados, olives, walnuts and liquid vegetable oils such as soybean, corn, safflower, canola, olive and sunflower.

Both polyunsaturated and monounsaturated fats may help improve your blood cholesterol when you use them in place of saturated and *trans* fats.

Trans Fat:

Trans fats (or trans fatty acids) are created in an industrial process that adds hydrogen to liquid vegetable oils to make them more solid. Another name for trans fats is "partially hydrogenated" oils. Trans fats are found in many fried foods and baked goods such as pastries, pizza dough, pie crust, cookies and crackers.

You can determine the amount of trans fats in a particular packaged food by looking at the Nutrition Facts panel. Companies have to list any measurable amount of trans fat (0.5 grams or more per serving) in a separate line in the "Total Fat" section of the panel, directly beneath the line for "Saturated Fat." This means if a food package states 0 gram of trans fats, it might still have some trans fats if the amount per serving is less than 0.5 g. Make sure to check the ingredients list for partially hydrogenated oil.

Sugars

Sugar is a carbohydrate that occurs naturally in various forms in all living things. In its natural form, sugar, as found in the sugar cane or sugar beet, is combined with a large amount of fiber, and also contains iron, potassium, calcium, B vitamins, etc.. These nutrients are needed to digest the sugar that is in the sugar beet or sugar cane, however white sugar has none of these.

When we eat sugar or starch our body breaks it down into simple sugar and the blood then carries it to the cells of the body. For this simple sugar to enter the cells it needs insulin and chromium, but if you have eaten only **fructose** sugar (the good kind that is found in fresh fruits and not from corn), no insulin is needed for the sugar to enter the cells. Refined sugar (**Sucrose**) drains out the mineral salts of the blood, bones, and tissues. It causes hyperactivity and dental cavities. It causes obesity, diabetes, low blood sugar, high blood pressure, duodenal ulcers, fatty livers, coronary and vascular disease, gout, dermatitis, and cancer.

Honey is a monosaccharide which does not over-stimulate the pancreas. Sugar also must undergo digestion, a process that changes it into simple sugar; whereas, honey is predigested and takes a load of work off the stomach and pancreas. Of course, pure organic raw honey is better than what you buy at the local grocery store. Raw honey will in a short time crystallize because unlike commercial branded honey, it has not been heated to a high temperature and had all the enzymes destroyed.

References

1. www.heart.org
2. Wikipedia.org
3. www.webmd.com

Made in the USA
Las Vegas, NV
04 September 2021

29603711R00036